VAISHALI

Written by

KANHAIYA JEE ANAND, AMIE,MBA
SHARDA KUMARI, PGDM (Human Rights)
BEDATRI ANAND, B.ARCH
UTKARS ANAND, B.ARCH

Address : Flat no-603, Block-A, Astha Green City,
AIIMS Road, Phulwari, Patna, Bihar-801505

&

At - Hasanpur, Lakhisarai, Bihar-811311
Mobile No : 9204783656, 9263303481

Title   : Vaishali

Author   : Kanhaiya Jee Anand, Sharda Kumari,
               Bedatri Anand, Utkars Anand

Edition   : 1st (May, 2024)

ISBN   :

Copyright © 2024, All Rights Reserved by Author

Published by

TANEESHA PUBLISHERS | *A Venture by -*
PRACHI DIGITAL PUBLICATION

Regd. Add.: 254, Khuriyakhatta No. 10, Bindukhatta,
Lalkuan, Nainital - 262402, Uttarakhand, India
Website : www.taneeshapublishers.in
E-mail : taneeshapublishers@gmail.com
Phone : +91 845481 2712, +91 976041 7980

Printed by :
Manipal Technologies Limited, Bengaluru - 560001, Karnataka

DEDICATION

This real research comes to mind from the grace of
Budhaavtar Jagatguru Shankracharya, LORD Budha,
Acharya Sayaji Ubakhin, Acharya S.N.Goenka Ji,
Mangla baba. Acharya Niranjana Sinha Ji.

Special dedication to Vaishali Vipassana center Vaishali
Bihar, where we are attached to perform Vipassana
meditation regularly.

Special Dedication to our beloved krishna Devotee
Mother Smt.Draupadi Devi whose guidance brings me
to Vipassana Centre,Upnayan Sanskar, RSS training
,Bolbam Tirth, and chanting of Hare krishna hare
krishna krishna krishna hare hare,Hare ram Hare ram
rama rama hare hare at various ages.

INDEX

Sr. No.	Title	Page
1	Vaishali City	
2	Basic of Town Planning of Vaishali City	
3	Basic of Social Engineering	
4	Meaning of Vipassana	
5	How Vaishali in Vipasana-A Experience	
6	Conclusion	

VAISHALI CITY

BRIEF-

Budha Samyak Darshan and Museum is under construction in 72 acre Land which will create a Stupa in which relics of Lord Budha should be kept. This is enriched with a Meditation center, minimum of 200 staying of devotees and green park.

About Vaishali-

Vaishali in Bihar was one of the Buddha's favorite resorts and he visited it on several occasions. It was here that he had his famous encounter with the prostitute Ambapali, the incident is recounted in the Mahaparinibbana Sutta in The Long Discourses.

Another discourse he delivered here is the long but interesting Mahasihanada Sutta from The Middle Length Discourses. According to the Mahayana tradition the famous Vimalakirtinedesa Sutra was preached here too.

About a hundred years after the Buddha's Parinirvana the Vaishali city was the venue for the Second Council where hundreds of monks from all over northern India met together to settle a dispute about Vinaya rules and to chant the suttas together. The main things to see today are the famous lion pillar, the museum, the large Kharauna Lake, the Japanese temple and the stupa built over the Vijjians' one eighth share of the Buddha's ashes.

Where is Vaishali

Vaishali city is situated in the eastern Indian state of Bihar, around 55 km off Patna, the capital of the state. Vaishali district extends from latitude 25° in the North to latitude 85° in the East. The town, an important place for both the Buddhists and Jains, is well connected to other important cities in Bihar by road.

History of Vaishali

Believed to be the first republic in the world, Vaishali Bihar has taken its name from King Vishal of the Mahabharata age. He is said to have constructed a great fort here, which is now in ruins. Vaishali is a great Buddhist pilgrimage and also the birthplace of Lord Mahavira. It is said that the Buddha visited this place thrice and spent quite a long time here. The Buddha also delivered his last sermon at Vaishali and announced his Nirvana here. After his death, Vaishali also held the second Buddhist Council.

The great Lichchavi clan ruled Vaishali in the sixth century BC, and the empire extended up to the hills of Nepal. The Lichchavi state is considered to be the first republican state of Asia. According to the Jataka stories, (Buddhist story books giving the account of different births of the Buddha), Vaishali was ruled by some 7707 kings of the Lichchavi clan.

Ajatshatru, the great Magadh King, annexed Vaishali in the fifth century BC and after that Vaishali gradually lost its glory and power.

Pilgrimage Attractions of Vaishali Travels

Ashoka Pillar

The Lion Pillar at Kolhua, was built by Emperor Ashoka. It is made of a highly polished single piece of red sandstone, surmounted by a bell shaped capital, 18. 3 m. high. A life-size figure of a lion is placed on top of the pillar. There is a small tank here known as Ramkund.

Bawan Pokhar Temple

An old temple built in the Pala period stands on the northern bank of a tank known as Bawan Pokhar and enshrines beautiful images of several Hindu gods.

Buddha Stupa – 1

The exterior of this stupa which is now in a dilapidated condition has a plain surface. One-eighth of the sacred ashes of the Lord Buddha were enshrined here in a stone casket.

Buddha Stupa – II

Excavation at this site in 1958 led to the discovery of another casket containing the ashes of the Lord Buddha.

Shanti Stupa

On the south bank of the Coronation Tank built by the Buddh Vihar Society.

Kundapur (Birth Place of Lord Mahavira)

4 kms. It is believed that the Jain Tirthankar, Lord Mahavira was born over 2550 years ago. Mahavir is said to have spent the first 22 years of his life here.

Coronation Tank or Abhishekh Pushkarni, its water were believed to be sacred in the old days and all of Vaishali's elected representatives were anointed here before their swearing in.

Other Places of Pilgrimage

Chaumukhi Mahadeva, Harikatora Temple, Lotus Tank and Miranji-Ki-Dargah, Jain Temple etc.

Excursion

Patssna 55 kms. Turning over the pages of early Indian history one comes across the name of the pre-eminent city of Patliputra. Located at the site where Patna is today, this city saw the rise and fall of India's first major Kingdoms. The Third Buddhist Council was held here.

Other Attractions

Vaishali Mahotsava

Vaishali Mahotsava is held to celebrate the birth anniversary of the Jain Thirankar, Lord Mahavir on the full moon day of the month of "Vaishakh" (mid-April). A perfect occasion to click beautiful Vaishali photos.

Arts and Crafts

Several villages around Vaishali make delightful home made clay toys.

Sikki Work

The humble blade of grass is hand-woven into delightful baskets and mats. Lac Bangles. These handmade Lac Bangles from nearby city Muzaffarpur.

Vaishali is a beautiful town which is surrounded by the Tree of Mango, Lichi and Banana.

The Land of River Gandak. Sandy and Silty of Gangetic region is the base.

A Live Brahmin Land producing paddy, wheat, vegetable, Fruits, WaterMelon etc.

Vaishali derives its name from King Vishal of the Ramayana and Mahabharata age. Even before the advent of Buddhism and Jainism, Vaishali was the capital of the vibrant republican Licchavi state since before the birth of Mahavira (c. 599 BC), which suggests that it was perhaps the first republic in the world, similar to those later found in ancient Greece. In that period, Vaishali was an ancient metropolis and the capital city of the republic of the Vaishali state, which covered most of the Himalayan Gangetic region of present-day Bihar state, India. Very little is known about the early history of Vaishali. The Vishnu Purana records 34 kings of Vaishali, the first being Nabhaga, who is believed to have abdicated his throne over a matter of human rights and believed to have declared: "I am now a free tiller of the soil, king over my acre. " The last among the 34 was Sumati, who is considered a contemporary of Dasaratha, father of the Hindu god, Lord Rama.

Numerous references to Vaishali are found in texts pertaining to both

Jainism and Buddhism, which have preserved much information on Vaishali and the other Maha Janapadas. Based on the information found in these texts, Vaishali was established as a republic by the 6th century BC, prior to the birth of Gautama Buddha in 563, making it the world's first republic.

In the republic of Vaishali, Lord Mahavira was born. Gautama Buddha delivered his last sermon at Vaishali and announced his Parinirvana there. Vaishali is also renowned as the land of Ambapali (also spelled as Amrapali), the great Indian courtesan, who appears in many folktales, as well as in Buddhist literature. Ambapali became a disciple of Buddha.

A kilometer away is Abhishek Pushkarini, the coronation tank. The sacred waters of the tank anointed the elected representatives of Vaishali. Next to it stands the Japanese temple and the Vishwa Shanti Stupa (World Peace Pagoda) built by the Nipponzan Myohoji sect of Japan. A small part of the Buddha's relics found in Vaishali have been enshrined in the foundation and in the chhatra of the Stupa. Near the coronation tank is Stupa 1 or the Relic Stupa. Here the Lichchavis reverentially encased one of the eight portions of the Master's relics, which they received after the Mahaparinirvana. After his last discourse the Awakened One set out for Kushinagar, but the Licchavis kept following him. Buddha gave them his alms bowl but they still refused to return. The Master created an illusion of a river in space which compelled them to go back. This site can be identified with Deora in modern Kesariya village, where Ashoka later built a stupa. Ananda, the favorite disciple of the Buddha, attained Nirvana in the midst of the Ganges outside Vaishali.

Broadly we can say that VAISHALI is the LIVE CITY from last 4000

Years has following characteristics is as under-

1. Vaishali is the First City in the world which has Democracy in WORLD. This happened in 6th Century BC. World learned this Democracy technology from the VAISHALI.

2. Chaumukhi Mahadev is the very old temple of LORD SHIVA in the city. In shravan Month people take bath in Ganga and perform Abhishek to Mahadev.

At a distance of 2. 5 km from Basarh Bus Station, Chaumukhi Mahadev Temple is a sacred Hindu shrine located in Vaishali, Bihar. It is one of the historic Hindu temples in Vaishali, and among the well-known places to visit in Vaishali.

Chaumukhi Mahadev, or Chaturmukhi Mahadev, is a historic Hindu temple dedicated to Lord Shiva. Also known as 'Vikramaditya Chaumukhi Mandir', the temple houses a huge Shivling with four faces representing Lord Brahma, Vishnu, Shiva, and Surya. It is said that the four faces of the Shivalinga point towards the 4 directions.

While the construction time is unknown, the temple is believed to have been built during the 5th century. According to legend, the temple existed during the Ramayana period. Lord Rama, Lakshmana, and Sage Vishwa Mithra visited the temple while on their way to Mithila, the kingdom of Janaka. It is also believed that Buddha and Mahavir stayed in the shrine. Chaumukhi Mahadev Temple is the mid-point of Kashi Vishwanath Mandir, and Baidyanath Dham (Deoghar).

This sacred shrine attracts many tourists and pilgrims alike. The footfall increases on all Mondays, and on Maha Shivaratri. The whole temple is beautifully decorated and devotees start visiting the temple from early hours on this auspicious day.

Timings: 6 AM - 6 PM

3. ABHISHEK PUSHKARNI

Abhishek Pushkarni

Abhishek Pushkarni of Vaishali was a sacred tank for the Lichchavis. The water of the tank was considered to be holy during the old century and was used by Lichchavis to anoint Vaishali's elected representatives before their swearing in. Abhishek Pushkarni also called the 'Kharauna Tank' or 'Coronation Tank', is considered to be a holy tank having tremendous healing powers in the ancient times. The Lichchavi stupa was located near Abhishek Pushkarni.

It was a 2600-year old pond or mini-lake; the water of which was used to sprinkle the coronation of head of ancient Vaishali Republic. This was the place where Amrapali was declared Nagarvadhu of Vaishali and was given the rank higher than that of the wife of the head of the republic.

Built on the south bank of the coronation tank is the Vishwa Shanti Stupa, which is a major desirability in Vaishali. This monument is one of the uppermost in the world and has been built in collaboration with the Japanese government. Other places of interest near the Abhishek Pushkarni are 'Chaumukhi Mahadeva', 'Harikatora Temple', 'Lotus Temple' and 'Miranji-Ki-Dargah'.

4. BAUNA POKHAR

Bauna Pokhar Temple is constructed using stone. Interior of the temple has beautiful images of Hindu Gods and Goddesses.

A unique characteristic of this temple is that a large number of Hindu gods are enshrined at one place.

This collection of different idols is made of black basalt, dating back to the Guptas and Palas. Also, a four headed Shiva Lingam is enshrined inside the temple.

Bauna Pokhar Temple is one of the most important places for the Hindu community's people in Vaishali. Not only is this temple significant for religious reasons, but also historical reasons.

The entire temple is full of different idols, which are quite beautiful. The most famous idol located inside the temple is the Shivalinga, which was created using black Basalt.

You will notice that the carvings of the idol are exceptionally well crafted. There is a stone edifice situated in the Bawan Pokhar Temple, which belongs to the medieval era.

The temple was constructed during the reign of the Pala dynasty.

Even if you are not religiously inclined, you will find this temple quite fascinating.

Apart from its beauty, the sheer archaeological importance of the temple is quite impressive.

King BALI PERFORMED YAGYA at Bauna Pokhar Temple and LORD BAWAN MAHARAJ asked the three leg LAND from the KING and King performed the Duty.

In Ram Navmi there was a huge crowd celebrating the ram navmi beside the Bauna Pokhar and in Temple

At a distance of 2 km from Basarh Bus Station, Bauna Pokhar Temple is an ancient Hindu temple located in Vaishali, Bihar. Situated on the banks of Bauna Pokhar, it is one of the historical temples in Bihar, and among the well-known places to visit in Vaishali.

Bauna Pokhar Temple or the old temple of Vaishali is dedicated to several gods. Built during the Pala period, Bauna Pokhar Temple has a unique architectural design built predominantly using medieval era architecture.

The beautiful images of Hindu gods and goddess adorn the walls of the temple and they are a salient feature of the temple.

In this temple, a big number of Hindu deities have been enshrined in one place and they all are worshiped collectively.

The Bauna Pokhar temple houses a rich collection of black basalt images dating back to the Gupta and Pala period.

Devotees will also get to offer prayer to a four-headed Shiva Linga found buried in the temple area. Not only Hindus, but people from other religions also visit this temple due to its mythological importance.

All Hindu festivals are celebrated here with great enthusiasm that lures a huge number of devotees.

Timings: 6 AM - 6 PM

5. HARIKATORA TEMPLE is located in Vaishali of Bihar. It is believed to have been built during the Gupta period.

Hariktora Temple is located in Vaishali, Bihar.

It is believed to have been built during the Gupta period.

This temple was built by a great saint Khaki Baba in about 1804-05.

The main point here is an image of Lord Kartikeya made of black stone, which is in a sitting posture on a peacock.

This temple is now in dilapidated condition. Bawan Pokhar Temple is nearby.

6. VISHWA SHANTI STUPA

This stupa is a symbol of peace and love and enshrines the relics of Buddha in its foundation and top.

Vaishali is the place where Buddha preached his last sermon before his Nirvana. The Vishwa Shanti Stupa is erected according to the teaching of the Saddharma Pundarika Sutra (The lotus Sutra) to disseminate love and peace and to create "The pure Land" on the earth.

The construction of the stupa all over the world was initiated by the most Ven. Nichidatsu Fuji Guruji, after seeing the tragedy of atomic bombs in Hiroshima and Nagasaki of Japan, at the end of World war 2. The Vishwa Shanti Stupa, Vaishali has been built by Nipponzan Myohoji and Rajgir Buddha Vihar Society. Through contributions of devotees in India and Japan, The Lord Buddha's relics have been enshrined on the foundation and on the top of the stupa.

7. VISHALGARH FORT

At a distance of 2 km from Basarh Bus Station, Raja Vishal ka Garh is an ancient fort located in Vaishali, Bihar. It is one of the historical forts in Bihar, and among the must include places in Vaishali tour packages.

Also known as Vaishali Garh, Raja Vishal Ka Garh is said to be the ancient parliament house, where around seven thousand representatives used to gather to discuss political affairs. A protected monument and maintained by the Archaeological Survey of India (ASI), the place has a huge historical significance believed to be existing since the time of the Vajjis and the Lichchavis.

Known as the 'Mother of Parliament in Bihar', Raja Vishal ka Garh is a huge dome spanning about a kilometer, containing looming walls about 2 meters high. A moat surrounds the corners of the towers, and the building is known to have been King Vishal's parliament. Excavations at the site have established the presence of human settlement in 185-73 BC together with artifacts dating back to 600 BC. Gold coins, precious jewels, terracotta figurines, utensils, and deer horns were some major items discovered here. The site has also revealed traces of a drainage system and objects from the Gupta, Kushan, and Shunga periods.

8. CHAMGADAR PED (BAT'S TREE)

There was an old banyan tree, one kilometer south of Vishalgarh where hundreds of huge bats were hanging from its branches. Locals said these bats had made this tree their home for hundreds of years.

There were many trees but bats were visible on a particular tree only. No one knows the mystery of these bats but tourists are told about this tree and its story.

9. MAYA MIR SAHEB'S SHRINE-

Basadh village was nearby through which we would go to the shrine of Kazi Miran Sutari. Kazi Saheb was a famous saint and the shrine belonged to him. The shrine was 600 year old and a disputed place. Disputed place?

10. RELIC STUPA OF LORD BUDDHA

Buddha Relic Stupa, enshrining one of the eight parts of the mortal remains of Lord Buddha after he attained Mahaparinirvana.

The Buddha Relic Stupa was built by Lichhavis as a mud-stupa in the 5th century BC. The stupa was later discovered in an archaeological excavation carried out under the aegis of Patna-based K. P. Jayaswal Research Institute during 1958-1962. The relic casket excavated from the core of the stupa contained the holy ashes of Lord Buddha mixed with earth, a piece of conch, pieces of beads, a thin golden leaf and a copper punch-marked coin. The casket was brought to Patna Museum in 1972.

11. Ashok pillar and the birthplace of Lord Mahavira-Vasokund on the right-

ASHOKA PILLAR

Ashoka Pillar with lion capital of all the Ashoka Pillars that I have seen, this is probably the best-preserved. Though the famous polish of the pillars can no longer be seen. There are no inscriptions on this pillar. But the lion sits very elegantly on the capital and the rest all features of a typical Ashoka pillar-like inverted lotus are there. There is a swastika-shaped monastery that has been recently unearthed, along with a few tanks. The complex is a typical Buddhist complex, with thousands of votive stupas. v And small shrines spread across the complex.

Picture of the Ananda Stupa constructed in the ancient city of Vaishali, India, with relics of Buddha's attendant monk and cousin Ananda. Also, here is one of the best preserved columns erected by the emperor Asoka, with a lion statue on top.

Excavations

Excavations are being carried out in one part of the complex and new discoveries are being made every day. Precious stones, beads, seals, terracotta figurines, etc have been excavated from this complex, including a crowned monkey. Monkey adds to the story of the place where they not only gave honey to the Buddha but also dug a huge seven-layered tank for him. Like Nalanda, we could see some carved bricks here and there peeping out of the ruins.

Vaishali – Birthplace of Lord Mahaveer

Birthplace of 24th Jain Teerthankar Lord Mahaveer

Birthplace of 24th Jain Teerthankar Lord Mahaveer
It is the birthplace of Lord Mahavira, the founder of Jainism.

Unfortunately, his birthplace is only a small space with a signboard telling you that this is the place where he was born. In the background is an unfinished structure of an intended temple. Which we were told is under dispute and has been in that state for quite some time. Jain temples are rich and beautiful everywhere. Ironically this place seems to be completely ignored. There is an institute for research on Jainology that has an old but beautiful library.

12. Ramchaura Mandir

Ramchaura Mandir is a temple located near Vaishali, which is pretty significant for the Hindu community. By the name of the temple, you can guess that it is dedicated to Lord Ram. According to local folklore, the temple existed during the time of Ramayana. If you want to see the full glory of the temple, try to visit Vaishali during the time of Ram Navami. The temple gets decorated quite beautifully during Ram Navami, and tourists from all over the world flock there to soak in the ambiance.

It is believed that Lord Ram visited the area while returning from Janakpur. Inside the temple, you will note, that devotees are worshiping footprints. It is believed that those footprints are of Lord Ram.

13. BAITHAKJI HAJIPUR

There are 84 Baithaks in India, and all of them are dedicated to Shri Mahaprabhuji or Swami Vallabhacharya. If you visit Vaishali, you must visit the Baithak located in Hajipur as it is one of the most important places for the Vaishnavism sect in India. Before exploring the Baithak, you must know, Swami Vallavacharya was the founder of a particular sect of Vaishnavism named Pushtimarg. He is quite famous worldwide as he explored the entire world thrice by foot to spread the preach ing of Vaishnavism.

In the Baithak, located in Hajipur, you will get to see the shrine. Not only the people of the Pushtimarg sect but also people from other religions visit the Baithak. The entire site is relatively peaceful and a great place to clear your mind.

14. VAISHALI MUSEUM

Vaishali Museum displays antiques found during the excavation of ancient Vaishali. Established by the Archaeological Survey of India in the 1971 the museum showcases prized possessions of a Buddha sculpture belonging to Pala period in which he is adorned with a beautiful crown, splendid necklaces and other ornaments.

There is a remarkable headless sculpture of Buddha in Bhumisparsha mudra. Amongst the exhibits is an extraordinary collection of antiques by a local villager, which belongs to the pre-independence era. These were donated to the museum.

Sculptures of Vishnu and Uma Shankar are present in the museum and there are figures of human beings and animals like monkeys, snakes, horse, bulls, etc. The museum has over 2000 antiques showcasing the medieval cultures and the reign of Mauryas, Guptas, Kushans and Sanga.

15. KESARIA

The Place of ANAR KALAM who was the Ist GURU of BUDHA.

World Tallest Buddhist Stupa in Kesariya, Bihar, India. Commemorating the Kalama Sutta and the giving of Buddha's bowl to the Licchavis before Leaving the WORLD.

Kesariya stupa is a Buddhist stupa in Kesariya, located at a distance of 110 kilometres from Patna, in the Champaran district of Bihar, India. The first construction of the Stupa is dated to the 3rd century BCE. Kesariya Stupa has a circumference of almost 400 feet and raises to a height of about 104 feet.

16. VIETNAM MAHAPAJAPATI NUNNERY, VISHWASHANTI PAGODA ROAD, VAISHALI - 844128

The Vietnamese temple in Vaishali. This is an important city because the Buddha visited several times and it was here that he announced his impending death. One of the eight original relic stupas was constructed here. During the ongoing Pariyatti pilgrimage, the group stayed two nights here hosted by loving and kind nuns.

Buddha gave instructions for Ananda to recite Ratana sutta.

Dhamma vaishali Vipassana Meditation Center-

The Vaishali Vipassana Center is located in Vaishali district of Bihar, Eastern India. The Vipassana Center offers ten day residential Vipassana seminars in the tradition of Sayagyi U Ba Khin as taught by Shri Satyanarayan Goenka.

17. SATI STHAN LAL GANJ VAISHALI

Satisthan Lalganj Vaishali a famous place in Vaishali, where a Sant Serving the temple namely Sant Mangla Baba who has power of -Ast Sidhi Nav Nidhi ke Data Aswar din Janki Mata.

Life will be meaningful only by following the path of religion: Jai Mangala Baba.

If a person does good work in life then it does not take long for his luck to change. If we follow the path of religion and accept good deeds, then the lines written on the palm also become correct. These views were expressed by the famous saint Jaimangla Baba from Jaimangla Dham located in Begusarai district of Bihar. Addressing the devotee gathering organized at Bistupur Q Road, he said that if a man imbibes patience, he can easily overcome even the biggest adversity. To face any situation, a man must develop strong willpower within himself. Jayamangala Baba further said that the question arises how will this happen? How will the willpower be strong? How will you get patience? There is a simple solution to this. Be optimistic. Keep your thinking positive. Keep yourself away from negative actions or talks. Having faith in God, involve yourself in religious activities. Became the bearer of the eternal values passed on from our ancestors. If a person starts implementing these things then good days will start coming in his life. Problems will start going away. Happiness will start knocking in the house. He advised the devotees to embrace good things themselves and also inspire their family members or others to do the same. It is possible that initially people may ignore what you say. But don't be afraid of this, you will get good results from it. The only requirement is that you should not let patience and restraint go away from you under any circumstances.

18. NANAK SHAHI GURUDWARA-

Lalganj of Vaishali has a priceless heritage of Sikhs, also a center of faith for Hindus, know its story.

Vaishali district, an important center of Buddhist and Jain religions, also holds an important place for the people of Sikh religion. Nanakshahi Gurudwara located in Lalganj, Vaishali is one such holy place which is a center of faith for Sikhs as well as Hindus.

Nanakshahi Gurudwara located in Lalganj, Vaishali. Awakening Lalganj (Vaishali), Samvad Sutra. Lalganj of Vaishali district is an unknown, sleepy, seemingly ruined town, but time has buried some priceless heritage gems in the pages of its history. One of these, Nanak Shahi Gurudwara located in Repura, is still brightening the pride of Lalganj despite its poor condition even today. You will be shocked to know about this wonderful cultural historical heritage, which is dilapidated due to encroachment, government neglect and neglect by the enlightened people who are deprived of their own glorious heritage. The painful reality is that even the Tourism Department never felt the need to look into this. That is, Purushaal, otherwise his body would have been destroyed. It would have developed into an unmatched religious historical tourist destination, and would have added to the beauty of Lalganj. After gathering information about this, we came to know that we are unaware of the history of this amazing heritage.

(Samadhi place of saints located in Gurudwara premises) Six saints including one Jinda took Samadhi here.

Nanak Shahi Gurdwara, spread over about four acres and housing the tomb of six saints, is the center of faith not only for Sikhism but also for Hindus. It is believed that whoever bowed his head with a true heart in this

Gurudwara, which has a history of about four hundred years, his wishes were fulfilled. This is the reason why even today people of the Sikh community from every corner of the country keep visiting this Gurudwara. Presently this Gurudwara is operated by Patna Takht Sri Harmandir Sahib.

Basic of Town Planning of Vaishali City

New Stupa construction is in progress in Vaishali, where relics of lord Budha should be kept. This was also constructed the meditation hall, Library, Math and administration building such that devotee of other country should reach here for stay and will perform the anapana and Vipassana meditation.

Vipassana Research Institute or some other can get this holy place for Anapana and Vipassana Meditation.

Already various Maths are available in Vaishali City.

Following Methodology required to Develop the Tirth City Vaishali is as under-

1. Identify the area 50kmx50km as a Tirth City Vaishali.
2. Provide Boundary wall all around.
3. Provide four Gate as per Temple Architecture.
4. Identify the various village situated in around.
5. Identify the entering people to provide Identity cum entry card who is entering the Tirth City either alone or in group with vehicle.
6. Identify the various temple, Nunary, Stupa, Institution, house of Lord Mahavira.
7. Restrict construction of Hotel in area.
8. Math cum Mandir should be promoted in this area.
9. All Budhist centre, Temple should be allowed to construct the Math with Mandir to facilate the person coming from the other country.

10. Internatinal airport should be developed with various Math near by to accomodate the people coming from the other country.

11. No commercial activity should allowed in side the Tirth city which producing unwanted sound, disturbing air quality, expansion of heat, taste of water and smell of Land.

12. Panchsheel should be compulsory followed in Tirth city.

13. Avoid unwanted construction in Tirth City such as houses should not allowed more than G+2.

14. Ensure the work to all permanent inhabitant in various Institution, Temple, Math and other agriculture and service area.

Every Villagers must get permanent work somewhere inside the Tirth City.

Basic of Social Engineering

World and every element in the world is the formation and combination of 9 elements: Earth, Water, Light, Wind, Ether, Time, Space, Mind and Soul.

Only one mission of every creature's life is to be in Mangal Maitri for 24x7x365x various years.

Indian social Engineering depends on the following universal designation based on the acquired Magal Maitri.

By Birth there is only three caste is as under

1. Man

2. Women

3. Trans-Gender

Details

Caste is dependent on work.

Initially people were living in the jungle, For safety people started to live together.

Forest is the place where we can get everything which is required for life, that is food, water, wood etc.

Further when people started to live together they cleaned the jungle to safeguard, due to this we loosen food and others.

At the same time people started to find alternatives to food.

Maximum people started to keep cattle and ox some people started to get food from the trees like from palm , Khajur, Mahua etc.

Further people started agriculture where safety from the jungle is found out.

Further development takes place and various work is started to safeguard.

The man who leads the troop or group is previously called King now they are called Leader.

Every person in this world has no caste; it is depending on the work they define.

Once upon a time everyone was tribal, further development given the birth of Yadav , kurmi, Kishan, Pasi, Machhuara, etc.

Further development divides kings, Dom, Chamar, Vaidya, Sant, kahar pandit, Lohar, etc.

Further Leader, Engineer, Doctor, Lawyer , Accountant, Teacher , The people who follow paigambar calling muslim, people who follow jesus called christian, people who follow Lord budha calling buddhist etc.

We are all Human.

We have to follow the religion of Law of Nature and WE HAVE TO WORK TOGETHER TO SECURE OUR LIFE AS REQUIRED BY RUNNING SITUATION.

Working together needs Mangal Maitri meaning extreme positivity in mind.

Mangal Maitri is the prime requirement of society such that different people can work together.

But in the present day it is missing. We have a holiday to have FUN, while it is needed for SADHNA.

What is a Holiday?

Holiday is a Common day of Leave after continuous working so that people can get recharged. There is a Leave on Saturday, Sunday, what is the use of this Holiday.

People travel here and there and enjoy LIFE which is not only disturbing the Peace condition it also not suitable for the gain of ENERGY.

Next working day people are not interested in work.

In Present Development of society it is essential to have a public Holiday to perform the Sadhana not to spoil the day to enjoy.

Enjoy destroying the Mangal Maitri Condition.

Hence preferable Holiday for Country should be based on Sadhna.

Now the question arises, when we can perform Sadhna.

Right time is a junction of two seasons causing the effect of various viruses and diseases.

Hence following Leave should be organized in world for better health and prosperity is as under-

1. 4 Navratri/Upnayan Sanskar sadhna/Sangha Sadhna/Vipasana Sadhna/SEASON CHANGING SADHNA in ASIN(Rainy-Autumn/Winter), MAGH(Winter-Vasant)), CHAIT(Vasant-Summer), ASADH(Summer-Rainy) Amavasya to Dasmi -40 Days

2. Amavasya Sadhan-12 Days(A day when water percentage fall down from 72%, it needs a Sadhna to Water)

3. Purnima Sadhna-12 Days(A day when water percentage increases from 72%, it still needs a Sadhna of water to increase the energy in the human body.)

4. Holi and Holika/Vipasana Sadhna on Purnima Falgun & Chaitya Ist-1 Days

5. Diwali and Laxmi/Vipassana Sadhana Chaturdasi & Amavasya karthik. -1 Days

6. Uttarayan Kaalchakra(Changing of Movement of SUN)/Makar Sankranti/ Upnayan Sanskar Sadhna/Sangh Sadhna/Vipassana and Sadhna(5Jan-16Jan)-1 Days preferable on (Dev Uthni Ekadashi if it comes)For Expert-11 days and Special Sadhna from(21 December-16Jan)-27days. And Extraordinary Sadhna from (08 December-26 jan)

7. Dakshinayan Kaalchakra(Changing of Movement of SUN from Cancer to Capricorn)/Cancer or Karka Sankranti/Upnayan Sanskar Sadhna/Sangh Sadhna/Vipassana and Sadhna(5 July-16 july)-1 days preferable for Normal People on (Dev Sayani Ekadasi if it comes)For Expert-11 days and Special Sadhna from(21 June-16JJuly)-27days and Extraordinary Sadhna from (08 June to 26 July)

8. Chhath Vrat Suryopasana/Vipassana Kartik & Chaitya 4th, 5th and 6th day-6 Days

9. Independence (15th August) & Gantantra(26th Jan) Divas Sadhna/Vipassana-2 Days

Total of 76 Days of Sadhna for Normal People.

Or 74+11+11=96 Days of Expert SADHNA.

Or 74+27+27=128 Days of Special SADHNA.

Or 74+48+48=170 days of Extra ordinary Sadhna

In one year SADHNA of 76 days for normal people and 96 days for Expert People , 128 days for Special SADHNA for Rishi and 170 days of Extraordinary Sadhna for Rishi and Maharishi is a compulsory requirement to gain natural Energy to create the Country SMART.

This above Auspicious day is required to be in peace not to run the mike or unwanted gathering rather should be for SADHNA only.

Market should also be designed such that PEACE should not be disturbed.

Vehicle movement should be restricted. Vehicle should be allowed which does not create NOISE or SMOKE etc means only Electric Vehicle or Rickshaw or Walking should be allowed.

It is well known that from morning 2. 30AM to 4AM Nature performs the MEDITATION.

From 4AM to 6. 30AM-All Creatures and Human beings Performing the Meditation.

From 6. 30AM to 12AM-Working Period. Peace Conditions always increasing the Efficiency.

From 12PM to Sunset-Hard Work Period. Peace condition energies the Body to perform effectively. Mike sound, Sound Pollution should not allowed. Mike should allowed for VED KATHA YAGYA, UPNISHAD KATHA YAGYA, PURAN Katha YAGYA, Ramayan Katha YAGYA, GITA Katha YAGYA, if every family is agreed.

From Sunset to 8PM-Creatures returning from their work and discussing the day. This is the time of Collective Gayan, Music etc in one place. If peripheral all people agreed then Mike may ON.

From 8PM to 2. 30AM Rest and Sleeping Period. All Creatures returning home and taking rest and sleeping hence this is also the period of REST such as all creatures should gain the perfect SLEEP to energize their LIFE.

HENCE PEACE is essential to create the Smart Society.

TRADITION, DAVA AND DARU is an essential tool to reach a

healthy condition. Quantity is per the Peace Condition of Life.

Example-In Bihar region HARIA, MAHUA AND TARI is the common and traditional JUICES which is prepared in house to use such as keep the healthy body. Such as in Summer HARIA is very good for health and Mahua is a good juice for the Winter Season and Tari for every season.

Eating Water Rice in morning is a tradition of BIHAR for the Summer Season from Holi Festival and Eating Sattu in daytime is another tradition of BIHAR for Summer Season.

Eating Chura Dahi in the morning is a tradition of BIHAR for the Rest season other than Summer Season.

STAGES IN LIFE-

Maharishi - The sages who reach their higher level of Mangal Maitri are called Maharishis. Like Shankaracharya, Lord Budha etc.

Sage- Sage is the author of Vedic hymns, which is possible due to hundreds of penances and meditation.

Muni - One who attains knowledge by practicing spiritual practice and remaining silent. Like Jain Muni.

Sadhu - The person who performs spiritual practice is called a sadhu.

Saints - Peaceful people practice peace. practice the truth. Like Sant Ravidas, Kabirdas, Tulsidas

Ignorant - People who are incomprehensible because of ignorance and intense fickleness. Today people of these qualities are found in abundance.

Shudra - One who serves quietly. Mukti is confirmed if they follow quality otherwise due to fickleness next birth in Vaishya, Kshatriya or Brahmin/Diwana. There is no need of a Guru, the Guru of a Shudra is the real nature.

Vaishya - One who does business calmly. Mukti is confirmed if they are following birth discipline otherwise Development of spasticity, next birth in Shudra, Kshatriya or Brahmin/Diwana. Because of fickleness, the need for a Vedic teacher.

Kshatriya - Protector carrying fickleness. If quality is followed of birth mukti is confirmed but Vedic Guru is always needed because of extreme fickleness. Due to differences in birth quality, Next birth should be in Brahmin, Vaishya, Shudra or Diwana.

Brahman - The storehouse of knowledge, penance and meditation full of playfulness. And in the end engage in service. Mukti is confirmed if they follow birth quality otherwise Next birth in Brahmin, Diwana or Shudra . Brahmin needs Continuous a Vedic Guru because of extreme fickleness.

Diwana - People full of fickleness and ignorance are engrossed in their mite. Lack of concentration, uncontrollable wandering and thinking is their work. Roaming life, next birth Brahman or Kshatriya or attainment of salvation.

The constant need of a Vedic Guru to reduce the effects of excessive fickleness and ignorance.

AvidYagami - When the natural quality of birth changes due to the influence of society and ignorance of birth, then human beings become AvidYagami. Continuous need of Vedic Guru. Next birth Vaishya Kshatriya or Brahmin or Deewana is fixed.

There is no need for a guru for peaceful beings. Nature is their teacher. A Vedic Guru is needed to bring restlessness to peace.

To do business in the Vedic way, Vedic vocational education is fixed for all eighteen years.

Playfulness is necessary for the construction and protection of society and peace is necessary for ready love.

Maharishi and Rishi are knowledgeable by penance of Vedic secrets, and peace and meditation are necessary for Muni. And it is possible for everyone to become a saint by meditation and a saint by just peace. Ignorance is a tendency of man from birth, there is no need to do anything for it.

In Ayurvedic Sanatan Hindu India, only Maharishi is eligible for President as per unwritten constitution and Rishi, Sage and Sadhu for Governor and Sadhu and Saint for Prime Minister, Minister and Chief Minister. All the scholars should try to become the form of Muni. Rest is suitable for the person who is in Ignorance.

Birth is the cause of development of will in previous life. If cause will end Birth cycle will end. Nothing is permanent in the world, everything has to be destroyed.

Jatkarma on the basis of astrology is essential to each being while Upnayan Sanskar is not essential for the person who is pure Sudra(A person in always peace), Even Sudra also required Upnayan to understand life deeply and Vedic Education with meditation to reach a stage of PEACE as Sudra changing to Avidyagami due to social disharmony.

Marriage is a system which helps to create a peaceful, high morale, stable joint family to perform Business, Safety and Living peacefully.

Antyeshti is essential to perform on the basis of being desired, but destroying the dead body in Agni should be common while Water

Samadhi, Earth Samadhi depends on their condition of mental health, Social and personal and special requirements.

To destroy the attachment with the person it is essential to go for Agni samadhi. Mainly family people should follow agni Samadhi.

Sixteen Sanskar are predominant in Life.

MEANING OF VIPASSANA

Vipassana, which means to see things as they really are, is one of India's most ancient techniques of meditation. It was rediscovered by Gotama Buddha more than 2500 years ago and was taught by him as a universal remedy for universal ills, i. e. , an Art Of Living. This non-sectarian technique aims for the total eradication of mental impurities and the resultant highest happiness of full liberation.

Vipassana is a way of self-transformation through self-observation. It focuses on the deep interconnection between mind and body, which can be experienced directly by disciplined attention to the physical sensations that form the life of the body, and that continuously interconnect and condition the life of the mind. It is this observation-based, self-exploratory journey to the common root of mind and body that dissolves   mental impurity, resulting in a balanced mind full of love and compassion.

The scientific laws that operate one's thoughts, feelings, judgements and sensations become clear. Through direct experience, the nature of how one grows or regresses, how one produces suffering or frees oneself from suffering is understood. Life becomes characterized by increased awareness, non-delusion, self-control and peace.

The Tradition

Since the time of Buddha, Vipassana has been handed down, to the present day, by an unbroken chain of teachers. The current teachers in this tradition were appointed by the late Mr. S. N. Goenka, who was Indian by descent but was born and raised in Burma (Myanmar). While living there, he had the good fortune to learn Vipassana from his teacher, Sayagyi U Ba Khin, who was at the time a high Government official. After receiving training from his teacher for fourteen years, Mr. Goenka settled in India and was authorised by Sayagyi to begin teaching Vipassana in 1969. During his life he taught tens of thousands of people of all races and all religions in both the East and West. In 1982 he began to appoint assistant teachers to help him meet the growing demand for Vipassana courses. Before he passed away in 2013, he left behind a comprehensive system for training and appointment of future teachers in the tradition.

The word vipassanā is composed of two parts: vi, which means 'clear', and passanā, which means 'to see'.

Vipassanā therefore means 'to see clearly' or rather 'to see things as they are'.

Most often, however, vipassanā meditation is translated as 'insight meditation', referring to the final result of this clear seeing: insight into the true nature of things.

The History of Vipassana

Vipassanā has its origins in the Pali-Canon, the collection of Buddhist scriptures in which the teachings of the Buddha are written.

Although vipassanā meditation is not described as a separate technique, the scriptures do state how to develop an understanding of the true nature of reality, which is essentially the basis for vipassanā meditation.

From the 10th century onwards, however, the common thought in many Theravāda Buddhist countries was that gaining insight would be too difficult because of the gradual decline of the Buddha's teachings.

Monks increasingly focused on the development of morality and the study of the ancient texts.

Meditation moved more and more to the background of the Buddhist practice.

The revival of vipassanā meditation took place in Burma (now Myanmar) at the end of the 19th century.

A key role in this revival is reserved for the Burmese monk Ledi Sayadaw, who, based on in-depth textual study and his own meditative experience, emphasized that liberation was still possible.

Ledi Sayadaw taught that vipassanā meditation as a path to spiritual liberation is accessible to everyone, regardless of background or religious beliefs.

Important disciples in the line of Ledi Sayadaw were U Ba Khin and his successor S. N. Goenka, whose methods are still taught today.

Other important figures in the history of vipassanā meditation include the Burmese monk U Narada (also known as Mingun Sayadaw), who developed the "New Burmese Method" of vipassanā meditation in the early 20th century.

U Narada's most important disciple was the Burmese monk Mahasi Sayadaw, who, with the help of the Burmese government, opened several meditation centers for lay people to teach this vipassanā meditation method to the general public.

In recent decades, vipassanā meditation has gained popularity around the world, thanks in part to Western students who have attended retreats in the meditation centers of Mahasi Sayadaw or U Ba Khin.

Vipassana According To U Ba Khin and Mahasi Sayadaw

The two most prominent teachers of vipassanā meditation in the

Burmese tradition are U Ba Khin and Mahasi Sayadaw.

Although both teachers emphasize the importance of vipassanā, there are some differences in their approach.

U Ba Khin was a Buddhist lay teacher. He emphasized the importance of morality (sīla) in the practice of vipassanā meditation, and encouraged his students to live virtuous lives to create the right conditions for successful meditation.

He also taught that it was important to first develop concentration (samādhi) through the use of breathing meditation (ānāpānasati).

Then this concentration is then used to examine the nature of the mind and the body, in other words, for vipassanā.

Mahasi Sayadaw's approach to vipassanā meditation is more technique-oriented than U Ba Khin's.

He developed a method of vipassanā meditation in which mental and physical phenomena are noticed and labeled when they occur in the present moment.

This technique is designed to cultivate mindfulness and understanding of the impermanent and self-less nature of reality.

Thus, an important difference between U Ba Khin and Mahasi Sayadaw's approach to vipassanā meditation is the role of concentration.

U Ba Khin emphasizes the development of concentration as a prerequisite for insight, while Mahasi Sayadaw's lableing technique is designed to develop both concentration and insight simultaneously.

It was Mahasi Sayadaw's hope that the followers of his method would later deepen their concentration through samatha meditation.

Another difference is the emphasis on morality.

While both teachers recognize the importance of a virtuous life, U Ba Khin places more emphasis on morality as the basis for successful meditation practice.

Vipassana According to Us

As mentioned, the practice of vipassanā meditation is in principle not tied to a religious or cultural background.

Whoever you are, wherever you come from and whatever you believe, vipassanā can help you get a deeper understanding of the essence of life.

It is not withour reasons that vipassanā forms the basis for the modern secular mindfulness movement, in which parts of the method are completely disconnected from the original framework.

At its core, however, vipassanā is part of the Buddhist path of morality, concentration and wisdom.

And it is through this path as a whole that real understanding becomes possible.

To develop morality (sīla), practitioners are instructed to refrain from killing, stealing, sexual misconduct, wrong speach, and the use of intoxicants.

With this moral code of conduct, you cultivate an ethical life and create the conditions for strong concentration.

Concentration (samādhi) is developed through the practice of samatha meditation (concentration meditation), in which you focus your mind on a single meditation object.

The goal of developing concentration is to achieve ever deeper stillness and calmness.

In our opinion, this calmness is a prerequisite for practicing vipassanā meditation to the deepest level.

With morality and concentration as a foundation, insight can be gained by investigating the nature of reality.

Vipassanā meditation is this investigation.

With the acquired stillness and calm and with full attention you can observe, with ever increasing power, the continuous, lightning-fast process of the arising and decay of physical and mental phenomena, completely in the present moment.

The result of this investigation is wisdom, seeing from one's own experience the impermanence (anicca) of phenomena and the self-less character (anattā) of this process.

The Need for Concentration

As you can see, like U Ba Khin and Ledi Sayadaw, we emphasize for him the importance of morality and especially concentration as a condition for vipassanā.

We actually go further then these two great teachers.

The practice of vipassanā meditation requires a sustained and focused effort to be able to continuously observe the current moment-experience.

By nature, however, the mind is easily distracted and inclined to wander, trapped in the flow of thoughts and emotions.

Concentration allows the meditator to keep the attention on the moment-experience and examine it in complete silence and objectivity.

There are several techniques that can be used to develop concentration, such as focusing on the breath, a mantra, or visualizing a particular object.

We use the mantra buddho, a reference to the qualities of the Buddha (buddhānussati).

The most important underlying aspect of concentration is the ability to keep the mind one-pointedly focussed on your meditation object, for as long as you want, consistently and completely equanimous.

This is not a matter of taking a few minutes of deep breaths or spending a few days of a retreat on developing concentrating. For most people, this requires years of directed effort.

As much as you want to get started with vipassanā right away, first you will have to develop the ability of your mind to concentrate.

It is concentration that ensures that your consciousness is powerful, still and refined enough to see things as they are.

I. Learning of Anapana, Vipassana or Self control Meditation and Mangal Maitri from the age of 18 years to 25 years and Continuous practice of Self Control Meditation is a good method to develop the Mangal Maitri for 24x7x365xVarious Years.

TECHNOLOGY OF ANAPANA MEDITATION AND VIPASSANA TECHNIQUE WITH MANGAL MAITRI IN DISCIPLINED ASHRAM.

(Buddham Saranam Gacchami, Dhammam Saranam Gacchami, Sangham Saranam Gacchami)

GITA CHAPTER-VI

LORD KRISHNA TOLD ARJUNA TO PERFORM SELF DISCIPLINE YOG-

This Yog explained that watch the front of Inhaling and Outhaling and watch and understand the sensation outside and inside the body.

Lord Budha discovered and practices this technique and reached a stage of ULTIMATE Peace and teaches above technique around 45 years. The Technology is as under. -

He has a Residential course of 48 days and now it is of 10 days, 15 days, 20 days, 30days, 60 days and so. This is taught by their Assistant Teacher and helped by SEVAK nowadays under guidance of Acharya S. N. Goenka ji

Every Student has to perform the duty of SEVAK in different Courses.

The activity of Sevak is essential to develop the MANGAL MAITRI.

The Eightfold Path consists of eight practices: right view, right resolve, right speech, right conduct, right livelihood, right effort, right mindfulness, and right samadhi ('meditative absorption or union').

Division	Eightfold Path factors
Moral virtue(Sanskrit: śīla, Pāli: sīla)	1. Right speech
	2. Right action
	3. Right livelihood
Meditation(Sanskrit and Pāli: samādhi)	4. Right effort
	5. Right mindfulness
	6. Right concentration
Insight, wisdom (Sanskrit: prajñā, Pāli: paññā)	7. Right resolve
	8. Right view

Ashram discipline is compulsory and starts from 4am to night 9. 30pm.

DAILY ROUTINE-

4am- Wake Up Period

4. 30am to 6. 30am-Anapana Meditation/ Vipassana Technique Time

6. 30am to 7. 00am- Satvik Breakfast with 1 fruit

7am to 8am -Rest

8am to 11am-Anapana Meditation/ Vipassana Technique Time

11am to 11. 30am-Satvik Lunch

11. 30am to 1pm-Rest

1. 00pm to 4. 30pm- Anapana Meditation/ Vipassana Technique

4. 30PM to 5. 00PM- Tea/Ginger Soup/Lemon Juice Break.

5. 00PM to 6. 00PM -Rest

6 PM to 9PM-Anapana Meditation/Vipassana Technique

9 PM to 4AM- Rest

Follow the Panchsheel Discipline.

- Abstain from killing
- Abstain from stealing
- Abstain from sexual misconduct
- Abstain from wrong speech
- Abstain from the use of intoxicating substances that cause inattention

ANAPANA MEDITATION(Strictly Under Guidance of Guru)-

Just watch the incoming normal breath and outgoing normal breath. Technique is very simple, but tough to control, because mind is not staying a point for more than 10 second to 1 minute. Once it reaches to 1 minute to 10 minute means life will get the direct energy from Nature.

- Practically it is difficult to make concentration on Breath, hence Lord Budha suggested an idea of Bhaw, there are three Bhaw of our vision either in closed eye or in open eye that is a. Bhokta Bhaw, b. Drasta Bhaw and c. Sleeping Bhaw. and other Bhaw is called Samta Bhaw.

- If we are keeping vision in Drasta Bhaw, our sight or concentration automatically reaches the nasal starting point where we can watch the Incoming and Outgoing breath easily and we can maintain it easily for 1 minute to 10 minutes.

- Be like an Umbrella, Umbrella helping us from rain in Rainy Season and sun-ray in Summer Season.

- This is the technique to follow for 3 consecutive days to control mind on Inhaling and Outhaling.

- Day-0-Giving words to Teacher to Learn the Anapana Meditation Introduction and Introductory Classes. Understanding the Drasta Bhav and Bhokta Bhav and learning to concentrate on Nasal starting place.

- Day-1 Practice to keep concentration in front of Nasal point. Lesson to Learn the technique to watch the Inhaling inside the Nasal.

- Day-2 Practice to keep concentration of Inhaling inside the Nasal. Lesson to learn the Inhaling at Entry Point.

- Day-3 to 5 Practice Whole day and Evening: Giving words to Learn Vipassana from Teacher and taking lesson to watch the different parts of body and feeling sensation.

VIPASSANA TECHNIQUE (Strictly Under Guidance of Guru)

The 15th day session is the complete teaching, while initially the 10 day session is sufficient, after experience join the 15th day, 20 day, 30 day, 60 day session. This cures the human body and human becoming like Children. Children is the real GOD.

Watching the Sensation at every part of our body and feeling the sensation for 7 day. In 7th, 8th, 9th, 10th, 11th, 12th, and 13th days the human body becomes fluid like volatile and energy movement becomes very fast. It cures from ill health trouble. Details is as under.

- Day-3 Practice Whole day and Evening Giving words to Learn Vipassana from Teacher and taking lessons to watch the different parts of body and feeling sensation, Or practice the Anapana Meditation.

- Day-4, Watching Each part of the body for 1 minute and feeling happiness. Taking Lessons to concentrate on Sensible and Insensible parts of the Body, Or practice the Anapana Meditation.

- Day-5, Concentration on the Insensible part of the body more and understanding the Sense and no reply for any sense. Learn the technique to Concentrate to Parallel Organ like both side hand etc, Or practice the Anapana Meditation and Evening Giving words to Learn Vipassana from Teacher.

- Day-6, Concentrate to parallel Organ. Learn the technique to Concentrate from top to Bottom and Bottom to Top.

- Day-7, Concentrate from Top to Bottom and Bottom to Top. Learn the technique of Feeling of Flow of Energy from Top to Bottom and Bottom to Top.

- Day-8 Practice to Flow of Energy from Top to Bottom and Bottom to Top. Learn the Technique of Bhang Yog.
- Day-9, Practice to Bhang Yog, that is free flow from Top to Bottom and Bottom to Top. Learn the technique to understand the Vedna of Inhaling and Outhaling in different parts of Body with Bhang Yog.
- 10th day focussing on Vedana means inhaling and feeling air entering and outing to other parts of the body. Learn the Technique of sensation in Kaya means in the skeleton of human body with Bhang yog.
- 11th day focusing on Kaya means the whole skeleton and we are feeling the sensation in bone and inside of bones. Learn the technique of understanding of Chit sensation with Bhang Yog.
- 12th day focussing in Chit means whole chit and we are feeling the sensation in chit. Learning the technique to understand Sensation of Dharma and controlling of Dharma with Bhang Yog.
- 13th day focussing on Dharma and we are feeling the sensation of Dharma for the world with Bhang Yog. Learning the technique to understand the Mangal Maity Session.

MANGAL MAITRI

- 14th day is for Mangal Maitri day. and returning to the routine Life
- 15th day-End session after morning session.

HOW VAISHALI CITY IN VIPASANA - A EXPERIENCE

Bank of Gandak is the area of Brahmin. Vaishali was the Democratic state from 6th century BC, before the arrival of Budha. Democratic states have their own sheel of Upnayan before joining the Gurukul.

Vaishali is the Land in which plenty of Banana, Mango and Litchi tree is found. This three plant and tree is the symbol of Vishnu and Laxmi.

Paddy, Wheat, Gram, Barley, various flower, various vegetable is the main product of the Land.

Still Vaishali is mostly open, which causing natural Energy is surrounding all around.

We stay at Vaishali and performed Vipasana in very peace situation. Our feeling was very positive and observed that not even public performing the Vipasana at vaishali, the whole nature performing Vipassana, even tree performing vipassana, plant performing vipassana, land performing vipasana.

Land is also watching inner soul. tree is watching inner soul, plant is watching inner soul. Animal is also performing vipassana and watching inner soul.

Vaishali is a Smart city not village which never sleeping whole Vaishali is in Vipasana for 24x7x365xmore than 2500 year.

Our experience is as under

Course starting time is 4am and end time is 9pm, but our wakeup time was 2. 30am, when Enviornment/nature/GOD performing the meditation and this understood and really seen by naked eye.

Our observation was even after 9pm complete nature performing the Vipasana and living live for whole night.

The student who is performing the Vipasana naturally they are mixing with nature and whole body transforming and joining with nature.

Follower of Budha in Vaishali developed the various stupa like Vishwa Shanti Stupa, Vaishali Garh, Relic Stupa of Lord Budha, Kharauna Pokhar, Ashoka pillar, Kesaria tallest Stupa in world(Land of GURU Anar Kalam), Vietnam Mahapajapati Nunnery, Srilanka Ramaya Buddhist Temple, Dhamma Vaishali Vipassana Meditation Centre. , where people from various part of world reaching and performing the Vipassana and strictly following the Panchsheel and remembering to Maha Prajapati who changed to Bhikkhuni in Sangha and performed Vipasana.

Guru Shishya parampara still live and Bikhu and Bikhuni or devotee from world reaching here and performing Vipassana here, causing whole earth is in vipassana from last 2500 years.

On advice of Budha, Ananda recited the Ratan Sutta in Vaishali. The land where Anand took Parinirvan also.

Bawan Pokhar Temple, Chaumukhi Mahadev, Birth place of Lord Mahavira-Vasokund is another ancient identification of a holy Land.

Recently Construction of new Stupa is under Construction where Relic should be further kept for the LifeLong. New Construction also includes the various plenty of space for the Meditation Centre etc.

Vaishali is the Holy and even Ist Land where GOD is staying and performing Vipassana in early morning 2. 30AM to 4AM and Earth includes all creatures, Tree, Plant is Live and in Vipassana for 24x7x365 more than 2500 years.

CONCLUSION

The Vaishali Land itself in Vipassana is really something LIVE. Live River Gandak with white sand is the symbol of Brahmin soil, Plantation of Banana, Mango, Litchi is the product of holy Brahmin and Mother of Democracy land.

The water of Kharauna Pokhar is auspicious and has special energy to keep Vaishali really Smart in all respects where Bikhu and Bikhuni come from various parts of the world and perform Vipassana in Panchsheel.

We will expect Government should not indulge to destroy the naturality of the Vaishali such that GOD should forever stay and perform Vipassana in early morning 2. 30AM to 4AM and Earth includes all creatures, Tree, Plant should Live and be in Vipassana for 24x7x365 forever.